T0011933

NARUTO:
NINJA AND HERO

x2003

Kenny Abdo

Fly!
An Imprint of Abdo Zoom
abdobooks.com

abdobooks.com

Published by Abdo Zoom, a division of ABDO, P.O. Box 398166, Minneapolis, Minnesota 55439. Copyright © 2022 by Abdo Consulting Group, Inc. International copyrights reserved in all countries. No part of this book may be reproduced in any form without written permission from the publisher. Fly!™ is a trademark and logo of Abdo Zoom.

Printed in the United States of America, North Mankato, Minnesota.
102021
012022

THIS BOOK CONTAINS RECYCLED MATERIALS

Photo Credits: Alamy, AP Images, Everett Collection, fandom, flickr, Getty Images, iStock, Pond5, Shutterstock, ©cocamert p.4 / CC BY 2.0, ©Teppei Kiyoshi p.17 / CC-BY-SA, ©PlayStation Europe p.18 / CC BY-NC 2.0
Production Contributors: Kenny Abdo, Jennie Forsberg, Grace Hansen
Design Contributors: Candice Keimig, Neil Klinepier

Library of Congress Control Number: 2021940179

Publisher's Cataloging-in-Publication Data

Names: Abdo, Kenny, author.
Title: Naruto: ninja and hero / by Kenny Abdo
Other Title: ninja and hero
Description: Minneapolis, Minnesota : Abdo Zoom, 2022 | Series: Video game heroes | Includes online resources and index.
Identifiers: ISBN 9781098226954 (lib. bdg.) | ISBN 9781644947401 (pbk.) | ISBN 9781098227791 (ebook) | ISBN 9781098228217 (Read-to-Me ebook)
Subjects: LCSH: Video game characters--Juvenile literature. | Ninjas--Juvenile literature. | Sony Playstation video games--Juvenile literature. | Heroes--Juvenile literature.
Classification: DDC 794.8--dc23

TABLE OF CONTENTS

NARUTO

As a young ninja and shapeshifter, Naruto has fought his way to the top of video game stardom.

Naruto exploded in popularity around the world after his **debut**. The **manga**, **anime**, and video games have all sold in the millions.

PLAYER PROFILE

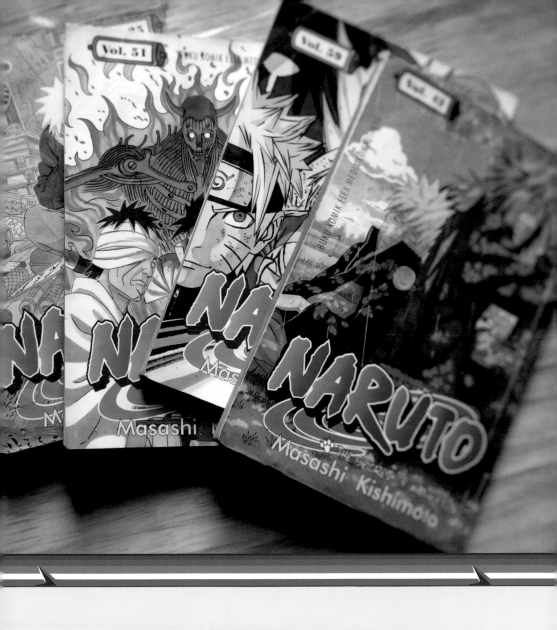

Masashi Kishimoto created a new **manga** series named *Naruto* in 1999. It followed a young ninja, Naruto, who lived in a fantasy world from Japanese mythology.

The **manga** became an instant success after it was first published! When the **anime** version was released in 2002, fans were exposed to Naruto around the world.

By the early 2000s, Naruto's fame had skyrocketed. He had conquered both comic books and cartoons. Now it was time to master video games.

LEVEL UP

Naruto: Clash of Ninja came out in 2003 for Japan and in 2006 for North America. There were only ten characters, but that was enough to keep fans coming back.

There were 10 *Clash of Ninja* follow-ups. *Naruto: Ninja Council* was announced in 2006. It had six **sequels** within five years, each as exciting as the last!

Naruto: Broken Bond came out in 2008. The **sequel** to *Naruto: Rise of a Ninja* quickly followed. Fans liked that the games used the voice actors and soundtrack from the **anime** series.

Naruto: Path of the Ninja did well both in North America and Japan. Fans liked that the new storyline was different from earlier ones.

Naruto Shippūden: Ultimate Ninja Storm 3 is considered one of the greatest **anime**-based video games of all time. Part 4 quickly followed. It included the ability to switch characters during battle.

EXPANSION PACK

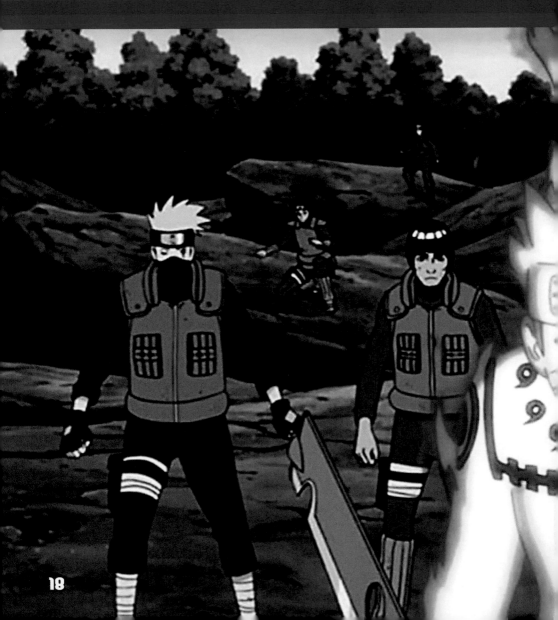

In total, Naruto has appeared in 72 volumes of graphic novels. He's also starred in 720 episodes of his own TV show and in 13 movies!

In 2019, Naruto became a **viral** meme. People would photograph themselves doing the "Naruto Run." The act itself is done by sprinting as fast as possible with both arms stretched out behind the back.

For more than fifteen years, *Naruto* has been one of the most popular **franchises** in the world. Proving he won't be outdone anytime soon!

GLOSSARY

anime – animation that comes from Japan.

debut – a first appearance.

franchise – a series of related works (such as video games or films) each of which includes the same characters or different characters that are understood to exist and interact in the same fictional universe with characters from the other works.

manga – Japanese comic books and graphic novels.

sequel – a video game that continues the story begun in a preceding one.

viral – a photo, video, or ad that is quickly shared throughout the internet.

ONLINE RESOURCES

Booklinks
NONFICTION NETWORK
FREE! ONLINE NONFICTION RESOURCES

To learn more about Naruto, please visit **abdobooklinks.com** or scan this QR code. These links are routinely monitored and updated to provide the most current information available.

INDEX